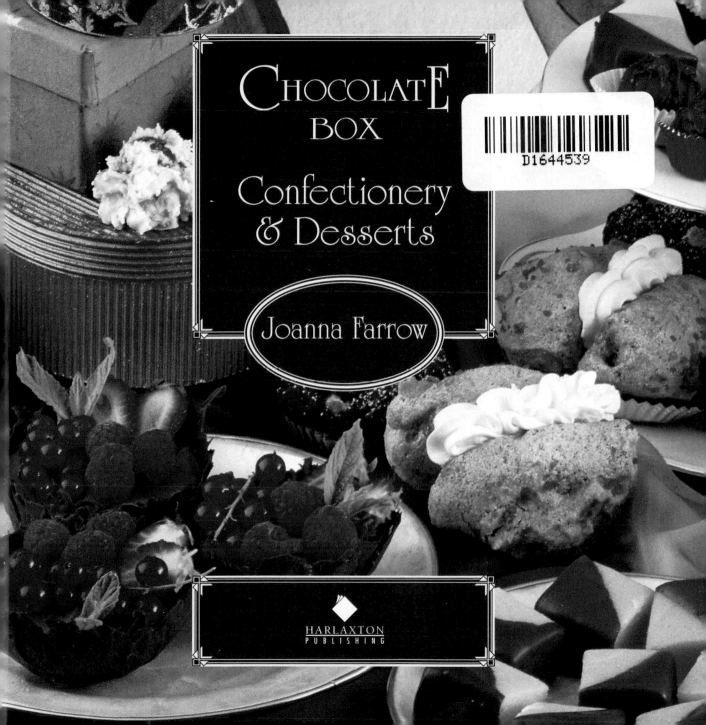

CHOCOLATE BOX

Confectionery & Desserts

Joanna Farrow

HARLAXTON
PUBLISHING

Harlaxton Publishing Limited   2 Avenue Road
Grantham
Lincolnshire
NG31 6TA United Kingdom
A Member of the Weldon International Group of Companies

First published 1994
© 1994 Copyright: Harlaxton Publishing Limited
© 1994 Copyright design: Harlaxton Publishing Limited

Publisher: Robin Burgess
Publishing Manager & Design: Rachel Rush
Editor: Alison Leach
Illustrator: Lyne Breeze, Linden Artists
Photographer: James Duncan
Home Economist: Sue Maggs
Stylist: Madelaine Brehaut
Typesetter: John Macauley, Seller's
Colour separation: GA Graphics
Printer: Mandarin, Hong Kong

British Library Cataloguing-in-Publication data
Title: Chocolate Box: Confectionery and Desserts
ISBN: 1-85837-143-0

Contents

Introduction
5
Decorative Ideas
6
Confectionery
10
Hot Puddings
30
Desserts
46
Ice Cream & Frozen Desserts
60
Index
71

The wonderful versatility of chocolate needs little introduction, and whether you are looking for a simple everyday pudding or an extravagant confection for a dinner party you will find many delicious chocolate treats in this book.

The desserts chapters include some good old favourites such as Steamed Chocolate Pudding with Apple and Raisin Topping (p.35) and Profiteroles with Glossy Chocolate Sauce (p.46) as well as some more unusual ideas. There are also 'freeze ahead' desserts which are especially useful at times when you have plenty of other cooking to do as they can of course be made well in advance.

Opposite: Decorative chocolate ideas.

The texture of chocolate lends itself to numerous decorations, whether melted and piped or just prettily shaped. The following ideas apply to special desserts, although some of the decorations can equally well be used on ice creams, mousses and chilled or frozen desserts.

Once made, chocolate decorations will keep in a cool, dry place for a couple of weeks. Interleave them with greaseproof paper (baking parchment) to prevent sticking.

Chocolate Chips

Use plain (dark), milk or white chocolate at room temperature. Using a sharp knife, cut the chocolate into very small pieces and scatter over chilled or frozen desserts.

Chocolate Cup Cases

These are used as containers for the Chocolate Colettes (p.22). Alternatively, use them as sweet (candy) cases for dipped fruits, or other small chocolates.

Melt a little plain (dark), milk or white chocolate (you will need about 125g/4 oz/4 squares to make 20 cases). Using the back of a teaspoon, spread a little chocolate over the base and sides of foil or paper sweet cases. Invert on a sheet of greaseproof paper (baking parchment) and leave in a cool place or chill until set. Peel away the foil or paper carefully from the chocolate.

Chocolate Leaves

Use non-poisonous, well-defined, pretty leaves such as rose, mint, lemon balm, scented geranium, bay or holly. They must be in good condition, clean and thoroughly dry to work successfully.

Melt a little plain (dark), milk or white chocolate (you will need about 60g/2 oz/2 squares to cover about 10 leaves, depending on their size). Using a paintbrush, paint the underside of the leaves with a thick layer of chocolate. Avoid letting the chocolate run over the edges of the leaf as this would make it difficult to peel away the leaf. Leave in a cool place or chill until set; then peel the leaf away carefully from the chocolate.

If the chocolate layer is too thin, apply a second coat before peeling away the leaf.

Dipped Fruits

Fruits like strawberries, grapes, cape gooseberries (ground cherries) and cherries look very attractive, dipped in chocolate, whether as a decoration, or to serve with coffee after dinner.

Melt a little plain (dark), milk or white chocolate (you will need about 60g/2 oz/2 squares chocolate to coat 15 fruits). Half-dip the fruits, one at a time into the chocolate; then let the excess fall back into bowl. Transfer the fruits to a sheet of greaseproof paper (baking parchment) and leave to set.

Feathered Chocolate Pieces

Melt 90g/3 oz/3 squares plain (dark) or milk chocolate. Melt 30g/1 oz/1 square white chocolate separately. Spread the plain or milk chocolate on to a piece of greaseproof paper (baking parchment). While it is still runny, use a teaspoon to drizzle the white chocolate over it. Run the tip of a cocktail stick (toothpick) or metal skewer through the chocolate to give a feathered finish. Chill until set. Peel away the paper and break the chocolate into irregular pieces.

Piped Chocolate Shapes

Melt a little plain (dark), milk or white chocolate and place in a piping bag fitted with a writing tube (tip). Alternatively, use a paper piping bag and cut off the merest tip. Pipe small shapes on to a sheet of greaseproof paper (baking parchment). (Do not make them too big or sprawling as they will be difficult to use.) Leave in a cool place, or chill until set. Peel the paper away carefully from the chocolate and use the shapes to decorate a chilled or frozen dessert.

Run-Out Chocolate Leaves

Trace the outline of small attractive leaves (ivy looks particularly good) on to greaseproof paper (baking parchment). Melt a little plain (dark), milk or white chocolate (you will need about 90g/3 oz/3 squares to make 10 leaves). Place a quarter in a piping bag fitted with a small writing tube (tip). (Alternatively, use a paper piping bag and cut off the merest tip.) Use the chocolate to pipe over the traced outline; then chill for 5 minutes. Using a small teaspoon or paintbrush, fill the centre of the shapes with the remaining melted chocolate. Leave in a cool place or chill until set. Peel the paper away carefully from the chocolate.

Home-made confectionery illustrates chocolate in its most luxurious form. Not only is home-made confectionery perfect for adding the finishing touch to a special occasion dessert, it will also be greeted with delight when served with coffee at a dinner party gathering.

Young chocolate lovers are not left out of the fun – there are pretty chocolate mice and colourful chocolate lollies, made at a fraction of the price of bought versions.

Most of the chocolates can be made up to a week in advance, provided they are stored in a cool place. Those including cream will keep for two to three days.

After Dinner Mints

Makes 25

1 packet Trebor mints
125g/4 oz/4 squares milk chocolate
125g/4 oz/4 squares plain (dark) or bitter (semisweet) chocolate

Draw a 25x12cm/10x5 inch rectangle on a sheet of greaseproof paper (baking parchment). Place the mints in a double-thickness plastic bag and crush with a rolling pin until virtually powdered.

Break the milk chocolate into pieces and melt in a heatproof bowl over a saucepan of simmering water. Remove from the heat and stir in the crushed mints. Spread on the greaseproof paper, just over the edges of the marked rectangle. Leave to set.

Melt the plain or bitter chocolate as above and spread quickly over the milk chocolate. Leave to set. Using a sharp knife, cut the chocolate into 5x2.5cm/2x1 inch rectangles. Keep in a cool place until ready to serve.

Cook's Tip

Take care that the milk chocolate has set completely before spreading with the plain. The plain chocolate needs to be spread fairly quickly so that it does not melt into the milk.

Previous page:
Chocolate after dinner selection, left to right, After Dinner Mints, Brandied Chocolate Cherries and Chocolate Praline Squares.

Chocolate Praline Squares

Makes 28

60g/2 oz/¼ cup caster (superfine) sugar
60g/2 oz/½ cup blanched almonds, roughly chopped
200g/7 oz/7 squares milk chocolate
90ml/3 fl oz/5 tablespoons double (heavy) cream
½ teaspoon vanilla essence (extract)
90g/3 oz/3 squares plain (dark) chocolate

Oil a baking sheet lightly. Place the sugar in a small, heavy-based saucepan with 45ml/3 tablespoons water. Heat gently until the sugar dissolves, then bring to the boil and boil until the sugar turns golden. Stir in the almonds and transfer to the oiled baking sheet. Leave to harden.

When brittle, place the mixture in a double-thickness plastic bag and beat the praline with a rolling pin until finely crushed.

Break the milk chocolate into pieces and place in a small saucepan with the cream and vanilla essence. Heat gently, stirring until smooth. Remove from the heat and leave to cool.

Moisten a 600ml/1 pint/2½ cup loaf tin (pan) and line with greaseproof paper (baking parchment). Beat the praline into the chocolate mixture and turn into the tin. Level the surface and chill until firm.

Break the plain chocolate into pieces and melt in a heatproof bowl over a pan of simmering water. Invert the milk chocolate slab on to the work surface (counter). Spread half the plain chocolate over one side of the slab. Leave for a few minutes to harden, then turn the slab over and spread with the remaining plain chocolate.

Chill until firm; then cut into 28 squares.

Brandied Chocolate Cherries

Makes 24

24 ripe cherries
2 tablespoons brandy
125g/4 oz/4 squares plain (dark) or bitter (semisweet) chocolate

Stone (pit) the cherries using a stoner or knife, keeping the stalks intact if possible. Place the cherries in a small bowl and add the brandy. Cover and leave to soak overnight in a cool place.

Break the chocolate into pieces and melt in a heatproof bowl over a saucepan of simmering water. Drain the cherries and dry on paper towels. Line a baking sheet with greaseproof paper (baking parchment).

Dip the cherries in the melted chocolate and transfer to the paper. Leave to set and serve, if liked, in foil sweet (candy) cases.

Variation
Use rum, amaretto or kirsch instead of the brandy.

Chocolate Mice

Makes 8
150g/5 oz/5 squares plain (dark) or milk chocolate
150g/5 oz/5 squares white chocolate
A little pink paste food colouring
1 liquorice 'bootlace'
1 strawberry 'bootlace'

Polish eight chocolate mice moulds with cotton wool. (If you have fewer moulds, make the dark and light mice in two batches.)

Break the plain or milk chocolate into pieces and melt in a heatproof bowl over a saucepan of simmering water. Melt the white chocolate separately. Reserve a tablespoonful of the white chocolate and stir a dot of food colouring into the remainder. Spoon into half the moulds and tap gently to remove any air bubbles. Cut the strawberry 'bootlace' into four 7.5cm/3 inch lengths and push into place for tails. Turn the plain or milk chocolate into the remaining moulds, using the liquorice 'bootlace' for the tails. Chill the moulds for 30 minutes or until set.

Invert the moulds on the work surface (counter) and tap to remove the mice. Using a fine paintbrush, paint the reserved white chocolate on the mice for eyes and noses.

Cook's Tip

Chocolate mice moulds are most widely available at Easter time from department stores and kitchen shops. You will find them in specialist cake decorating shops throughout the year. When colouring the white chocolate, make sure you use a paste rather than liquid colouring which would make the chocolate solidify. Alternatively, leave the mice white–they will look just as effective.

Chocolate Lollies

Makes 8

30g/1 oz sugarpaste
Red food colouring
175g/6 oz/6 squares milk chocolate
8 strawberry 'bootlaces'
Smarties (multi-coloured chocolate drops)
30g/1 oz/1 square plain (dark) chocolate

Draw eight 6cm/2½ inch circles, spaced slightly apart on greaseproof paper (baking parchment). Turn the paper over and lay on a baking sheet or tray. Arrange eight ice lolly sticks with the ends 2.5cm/1 inch inside each circle. Colour the sugarpaste red and shape eight round 'noses' and 8 'mouths'.

Break the milk chocolate into pieces and melt in a heatproof bowl over a saucepan of simmering water. Divide among the circles, spreading it out to the edges and being careful not to dislodge the lolly sticks.

While the chocolate is still soft, press the noses and mouths into position. Add Smarties for eyes. Crumple up the 'bootlaces' and position for hair.

Melt the plain chocolate and use to decorate the eyes with a small paintbrush. Leave to set.

Left: Chocolate fun ideas for children, Chocolate Mice and Chocolate Lollies.

Chocolate-Dipped Fudge

Makes 675g/1½ lb

450g/1 lb/2 cups granulated sugar
90g/3 oz/⅓ cup unsalted butter
150ml/¼ pint/⅔ cup milk
175g/6 oz can evaporated milk
2 teaspoons vanilla essence (extract)
90g/3 oz/3 squares plain (dark), milk or white chocolate to decorate

Oil an 18cm/7 inch shallow square baking tin (pan) lightly. Place the sugar, butter, milk and evaporated milk in a large, heavy-based saucepan and heat gently until the butter has melted and sugar has dissolved.

Bring to the boil and boil without stirring until a temperature of 116°C/240°F is reached on a sugar thermometer. (Alternatively, drop a little of the mixture into a bowl of iced water. It should form a soft ball when rolled between the fingers.)

Remove from the heat and add the vanilla essence. Beat with a wooden spoon until the mixture is thick and slightly grainy in texture. Scrape into the prepared tin and level the surface. Leave to cool.

Cut the fudge into small squares and remove from the tin. Transfer to a sheet of greaseproof paper (baking parchment), spaced slightly apart, and leave to dry out for 1–2 hours.

Break the chocolate into pieces and melt in a heatproof bowl over a pan of simmering water. Half-dip each piece of fudge in the chocolate, letting the excess drop back into bowl. Return to the greaseproof paper to set.

Right: Chocolate gifts, left to right, Chocolate Fudge, Fresh Cream Truffles and Chocolate Orange Logs.

Fresh Cream Truffles

Makes about 24   125g/4 oz/4 squares plain (dark) chocolate
125g/4 oz/4 squares milk chocolate
125ml/4 fl oz/½ cup double (heavy) cream
2 tablespoons Cointreau or Grand Marnier
Finely grated rind of 1 orange

To Decorate: 125g/4 oz/4 squares plain (dark) chocolate
125g/4 oz/4 squares white chocolate

Break the plain and milk chocolate into pieces and melt together in a heatproof bowl over a pan of simmering water. Remove from the heat and stir in the cream, liqueur and orange rind until smooth. Chill until fairly firm.

Using a teaspoon, take scoops of the mixture and roll these into small balls. Chill again until firm.

To decorate, melt the remaining plain and white chocolate in separate bowls. Dip half the truffles, one at a time, in the plain chocolate until coated. Transfer to a greaseproof paper-lined (baking parchment-lined) baking sheet. Touch the surface of each with the back of a fork to give a textured finish. Repeat with the white chocolate. Chill for up to 3 days before serving.

Variations
* Use rum or brandy instead of the orange-flavoured liqueur and omit the orange rind.
* Instead of coating in melted chocolate, roll the truffles in cocoa powder or finely chopped, toasted nuts.

Chocolate Orange Logs

Makes about 30   60g/2 oz amaretti biscuits (cookies)
125g/4 oz/4 squares plain (dark) chocolate
90ml/3 fl oz/5 tablespoons double (heavy) cream
Finely grated rind of ½ orange
1 tablespoon Cointreau or orange-flavoured liqueur
Cocoa powder for dusting

To Decorate: 60g/2 oz/2 squares plain (dark) chocolate
Cocoa powder and icing (confectioners') sugar for dusting

Place the amaretti biscuits in a strong plastic bag and crush finely. Break the chocolate into pieces and melt it in a heatproof bowl over a saucepan of simmering water. Stir in the cream, orange rind, liqueur and crushed biscuits, and stir until evenly combined.

Using hands dusted with cocoa powder, halve the mixture and shape into two logs, each about 1cm/½ inch wide. Chill until firm.

Break the remaining chocolate into pieces and melt it as above. Brush over the logs and then cut widthways into 2.5cm/1 inch lengths. Serve dusted with cocoa powder and icing sugar.

Double-Dipped Fruits

Makes about 30   8 cape gooseberries (ground cherries)
Small bunch of seedless black or white grapes
60g/2 oz/2 squares plain (dark) chocolate
60g/2 oz/2 squares white chocolate
125g/4 oz/1 cup strawberries

Pull back the skins from the cape gooseberries but leave attached. Separate the grapes. Break the plain chocolate into pieces and melt in a heatproof bowl over a saucepan of simmering water. Melt the white chocolate separately.

Line a large baking sheet or tray with greaseproof paper (baking parchment). Half-dip the fruits in the white chocolate and place on the paper. Chill for several minutes until beginning to set; then dip the fruits again in the plain chocolate, adjusting the angle so that some of the white chocolate still shows. Keep in a cool place until ready to serve.

Cook's Tip

Larger fruits such as wedges of peach, nectarine, apricot or mango look pretty drizzled with melted chocolate. Lay the wedges on greaseproof paper. Place the chocolate in a paper piping bag; snip off the end and 'scribble' the chocolate over the fruits.

Left: Double Dipped Fruits.

Chequered Chocolate Marzipan

Makes 300g/11 oz   225g/8 oz white almond paste
Pink or green food colouring
Icing (confectioners') sugar for dusting
90g/3 oz/3 squares plain (dark) or bitter (semisweet) chocolate

Divide the almond paste in half and knead a little pink or green food colouring into one half. Form each half into a 10x2.5x2.5cm/4x1x1 inch block. On a surface lightly dusted with icing sugar, cut each block lengthways into nine even-sized rectangles. Re-assemble the rectangles into two large blocks, alternating the colours on each to make a chequered pattern. Trim the edges to neaten if necessary.

Break the chocolate into pieces and melt in a heatproof bowl over a saucepan of simmering water. Place the almond paste rectangles on a sheet of greaseproof paper (baking parchment). Spread a little melted chocolate along one long side of each and chill briefly until set. Turn the paste so that the chocolate-coated sides are underneath, then coat the remaining sides with chocolate. Chill until set; then cut widthways into slices.

Cook's Tip

If the almond paste rectangles do not stick together easily, brush with a little water or melted apricot jam before assembling.

Coconut Kisses

Makes about 24   225g/8 oz icing (confectioners') sugar
60g/2 oz/¼ cup unsalted butter, softened
100g/3½ oz/1¼ cups desiccated (shredded) coconut
Few drops of pink food colouring

125g/4 oz/4 squares plain (dark) or milk chocolate to decorate

Sift the icing sugar into a heatproof bowl. Add the butter and 2 tablespoons hot water. Rest the bowl over a pan of simmering water and beat until the mixture is warm and runny. Add the coconut and stir until combined.

Transfer half the mixture to a separate bowl and beat in a little pink food colouring. Shape both mixtures into small oval shapes about 3cm/1¼ inches long and transfer to a greaseproof paper-lined (baking parchment-lined) baking sheet. Chill until firm.

Break the chocolate into pieces and melt in a heatproof bowl over a pan of simmering water. Place a quarter of the chocolate in a paper piping bag and snip off the tip. Drizzle the chocolate over half the sweets. Half-dip the remaining coconut shapes, one at a time, in the remaining melted chocolate, letting the excess chocolate drop back into bowl; then return the shapes to the baking sheet. Leave to set.

Left: Coconut Kisses.

Chocolate-Coated Peanut Brittle

Makes 300g/11oz   175g/6 oz/1½ cups shelled, raw peanuts
225g/8 oz/1 cup granulated sugar
125g/4 oz/¾ cup light muscovado sugar
60g/2 oz golden (light corn) syrup
30g/1 oz/2/3 tablespoons tablespoons unsalted butter
¼ teaspoon bicarbonate of soda (baking soda)
125g/4 oz/4 squares plain (dark) or milk chocolate

Oil a 28x20cm/11x8inch shallow baking tin (pan) lightly and line with non-stick baking parchment. Grease the paper lightly. Toast the peanuts.

Put the granulated and muscovado sugars in a saucepan with the syrup and 4 tablespoons water. Heat gently until the sugar has dissolved. Bring to the boil and boil rapidly until the temperature reaches 154°C/310°F on a sugar thermometer. (Alternatively, drop a little of the syrup into a bowl of iced water. It should form threads which are hard and brittle.)

Remove from the heat and dip the base of the pan in cold water to prevent further cooking. Stir in the butter, bicarbonate of soda and toasted peanuts immediately. Pour the mixture into the tin and leave for several hours until brittle.

Break the chocolate into pieces and melt in a heatproof bowl over a saucepan of simmering water. Remove the peanut brittle from the tin and place on a sheet of grease-proof paper (baking parchment). Spread half the chocolate over the brittle and chill until beginning to set. Turn the brittle over and spread with the remaining chocolate. Leave until set. To break the brittle into chunks, use a sturdy knife, tapping with the end of a rolling pin.

Cook's Tip

Wrap the peanut brittle in a plastic bag or cellophane, or store in a lidded jar as the brittle turns sticky when left exposed.

Rocky Roads

Makes about 450g/1 lb

6 white marshmallows
6 pink marshmallows
60g/2 oz/½ cup blanched almonds, chopped
30g/1 oz/3 tablespoons raisins
225g/8 oz/8 squares milk chocolate
60g/2 oz/½ cup flaked (slivered) almonds, toasted

Using scissors, snip the marshmallows into small pieces. Mix the chopped almonds with the marshmallows and raisins.

Break 175g/6 oz/6 squares of the chocolate into pieces and melt in a heatproof bowl over a pan of simmering water. Add to the marshmallow mixture and stir until combined. Transfer to a piece of greaseproof paper (baking parchment). Wrap the paper around the mixture, pressing it into a roll, about 3cm/1¼ inches thick. Chill until firm.

Melt the remaining chocolate as above. Scatter the flaked almonds over another piece of greaseproof paper. Spread the chocolate roll with the melted chocolate, then coat in the flaked almonds. Chill briefly until firm. Cut the roll widthways into slices.

Left: Chocolate-Coated Peanut Brittle and Rocky Roads.

Mini Chocolate Tuiles

Makes about 28   30g/1 oz/ 2 tablespoons unsalted butter
3 egg whites
100g/3½ oz/scant ½ cup caster (superfine) sugar
2 tablespoons plain (all-purpose) flour
1 tablespoon cocoa powder
½ teaspoon ground mixed spice (apple pie spice)
2 tablespoons double (heavy) cream
Icing (confectioners') sugar and cocoa powder for dusting

Line a large baking sheet with non-stick baking parchment. Melt the butter and leave to cool slightly.

Place the egg whites and sugar in a bowl and whisk lightly. Sift the flour, cocoa powder and mixed spice into the bowl. Add the cream and melted butter, and beat until smooth.

Place teaspoonfuls of the mixture on the baking sheet, spaced well apart and spread out slightly. (You will need to bake about 10 at a time.) Bake in a preheated oven at 180°C/350°F/gas 4 for 6-8 minutes until the edges are slightly darker in colour. Remove from the oven and leave for 1 minute before lifting the biscuits carefully over a rolling pin and leaving to set into crisp, curled shapes. Repeat with the remaining mixture.

Store in an airtight container and serve dusted with icing sugar and cocoa powder.

Cook's Tip

If the tuiles cool on the baking sheet before you have had time to shape them, return to the oven for a few moments to soften and then try again.

Chocolate Colettes

Makes 24   150g/5 oz/5 squares plain (dark) chocolate

Filling: 90g/3 oz/¾ cup pistachio nuts
175g/6 oz/6 squares plain (dark) chocolate
125ml/4 fl oz/½ cup double (heavy) cream
2 tablespoons amaretto liqueur or brandy

Break the plain chocolate into pieces and melt in a heatproof bowl over a saucepan of simmering water. Spoon inside 24 foil sweet (candy) cases, spreading evenly up the sides. Invert the cases on a greaseproof paper-lined (baking parchment-lined) tray or baking sheet and chill until set.

Chocolate Walnut Fudge

Makes about 575g/1¼ lb

125g/4 oz/4 squares plain (dark) chocolate, grated
60g/2 oz/½ cup broken walnuts, finely chopped
450g/1 lb/2 cups granulated sugar
60g/2 oz/¼ cup unsalted butter
90ml/3 fl oz/5 tablespoons evaporated milk

Oil an 18cm/7inch shallow square baking tin (pan) lightly. Place the sugar, butter and evaporated milk in a large, heavy-based saucepan and heat gently until the butter has dissolved and the sugar has melted. Bring to the boil and boil without stirring until a temperature of 116°C/240°F is reached on a sugar thermometer. (Alternatively, drop a little of the mixture into a bowl of iced water. It should form a soft ball when rolled between the fingers.)

Remove from the heat and leave for 2 minutes. Add the grated chocolate and walnuts, and beat with a wooden spoon until the mixture is slightly grainy. Scrape into the prepared tin and level the surface. Leave to cool.

Cut the fudge into small squares and remove from the tin. Transfer to a sheet of greaseproof paper (baking parchment), spaced slightly apart, and leave to dry out.

Variation

Add 30ml/2 tablespoons brandy, rum or orange liqueur to the fudge when beating in the chocolate.

Put the pistachio nuts in a heatproof bowl and cover with boiling water. Leave for 1 minute. Drain the nuts and rub between several sheets of paper towels to remove the skins. Reserve 24 of the best nuts and chop roughly.

Break the remaining chocolate into pieces. Bring the cream just to the boil in a saucepan. Remove from the heat and stir in the chocolate until it has melted. Spoon into a bowl and stir in the liqueur or brandy. Leave to cool slightly and then beat until peaking softly. Place in a piping bag fitted with a star tube (tip).

Pipe a little of the mixture into the chocolate cases and sprinkle with the whole pistachio nuts. Use the remaining mixture to pipe swirls on to each. Decorate with the reserved whole pistachio nuts.

Above: Chocolate Colettes in pretty sweet cases.
Next page: Chocolate Egg Selection, beautifully decorated to make perfect Easter gifts.

White Chocolate Clusters

Makes 200g/7 oz   125g/4 oz/4 squares white chocolate
60g/2 oz/½ cup unsalted peanuts, hazelnuts
or Brazil nuts, roughly chopped
30g/1 oz/3 tablespoons raisins

Break the chocolate into pieces and melt in a heatproof bowl over a saucepan of simmering water. Mix the nuts with the raisins and add to the chocolate, stirring very lightly until just coated in chocolate.

Line a baking sheet with greaseproof paper (baking parchment). Place teaspoonfuls of the chocolate mixture on the paper and leave to set. Serve in small paper cases.

Home-made Easter Eggs

A great variety of Easter egg moulds are available from specialist cake decorating and kitchen equipment shops. There are many different ways of decorating the eggs. They can be made using one type of chocolate or using two or three different ones. As a guide allow about 60g/2 oz/2 squares chocolate for a 6cm/2½ inch egg, 175g/6 oz/6 squares chocolate for an 11cm/4½ inch egg and 225g/8 oz/8 squares chocolate for a 12-15cm/5-6 inch egg.

Wash and dry the moulds thoroughly, and then 'polish' the insides with a little cotton wool.

Break the chocolate into pieces and melt in a heatproof bowl over a saucepan of simmering water. Spoon into the two half moulds, spreading up the sides with the back of a teaspoon. Place, face-down, on a sheet of greaseproof paper (baking parchment) and chill for 30 minutes. Spread with a second layer of chocolate and chill until set.

To remove from the moulds, ease the sides of the mould away carefully from the chocolate. Invert on a work surface (counter) and tap firmly to release the moulds. If the chocolate will not part from the mould, freeze for several minutes so that the chocolate contracts slightly.

To assemble an egg, lay one half on a cup or ramekin and brush the edges generously with a little more melted chocolate. Press the second half gently into position.

Cook's Tip

Try to work with cool hands, if necessary putting them in cold water for several minutes. When releasing the chocolate from the moulds, support the moulds in a tea-towel (dish cloth) so that the warmth of your hands does not dull the chocolate.

Variations

Filigree Eggs – Place a little white chocolate in a paper piping bag and snip off the tip. Drizzle wavy lines into each half of the mould. Chill for 5 minutes; then spread with the plain or milk chocolate quite quickly as the warmth of the chocolate will gradually soften the piped white chocolate. Chill and unmould as above. As a variation use plain or milk chocolate for piping and white chocolate for spreading.

Latticed Eggs – Make as for filigree eggs; piping the white chocolate in a lattice pattern.

Polka Dot Eggs – Make as for filigree eggs; piping dots of white chocolate into the moulds.

Decorating Easter Eggs

Once the Easter egg shells are made, there are various ways to decorate them prettily for presentation, from simple ribbon ties to detailed piping.

Ribbon Eggs – Place the egg in a ramekin or small dish to steady it. Place a dot of melted chocolate at the base and top of the egg over the join. Secure a piece of ribbon over the melted chocolate, covering the join around the shell. If liked, add a second ribbon around the 'waist' of the egg and finish with a small bow.

Shell Borders – For one large or two small eggs, bring 60ml/ 4 tablespoons double (heavy) cream to the boil in a small pan. Stir in 60g/2 oz/2 squares broken plain or milk chocolate until it has melted. Leave to cool; then beat until the mixture forms soft peaks. Place in a piping bag fitted with a shell or star tube (tip). Place the egg in a ramekin or small dish to steady it and pipe a row of shells over the join.

Dots and Dashes – Place the egg in a ramekin or small dish to steady it. Melt a little plain milk or white chocolate and place in a piping bag fitted with a fine writing tube (tip). (Alternatively, use a paper piping bag and snip off the merest tip.) Pipe clusters of dots or scribbled lines of chocolate over one half of the shell. Chill the egg for 5 minutes until the piping has set; then turn the shell over carefully and repeat on the other side.

Wrapping Easter Eggs

After the eggs are decorated and any piping has hardened, they can be arranged attractively in boxes or cellophane. Cut circles or squares of cellophane and use to enclose the eggs, tying the ends with lengths of ribbon. If using boxes, cover them with wrapping paper and line with crumpled tissue paper. Bought, decorated gift boxes or bags can also be used. Again, line them with crumpled tissue paper to cushion and enhance the egg.

This chapter contains a delicious selection of both old favourites and more unusual recipes, either to serve as a simple mid-week pudding or to grace a more elaborate dinner.

Mouthwatering hot chocolate sponges like the Steamed Chocolate Pudding with Apple and Raisin Topping(p.35) and the Chocolate Layer Pudding (this page) make perfect winter warmers. Pastry lovers can indulge in a Chocolate Meringue Pie (p.40), a rich Chocolate Walnut Pie (p.42) or an interesting variation on a flaky Almond and Chocolate Pithiviers (p.41) with an irresistible layer of chocolate sauce. Whatever your choice, do not forget to serve with plenty of pouring cream for the ultimate indulgence!

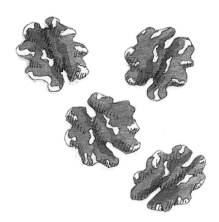

Previous page: Steamed Chocolate Pudding with Apple and Raisin Topping (p.35).

Chocolate Layer Pudding

Serves 5

125g/4 oz/½ cup unsalted butter, softened
225g/8 oz/1¼ cups light muscovado sugar
1 teaspoon vanilla essence (extract)
2 eggs, beaten
125g/4 oz/1 cup self-raising flour
4 tablespoons cocoa powder
Milk
Icing (confectioners') sugar for dusting

Grease a 1.4 litre/2½ pint/6¼ cup pie dish lightly. Beat the butter and 125g/4 oz/⅔ cup of the sugar with the vanilla together until light and fluffy. Beat in the eggs gradually, a little at a time until light and fluffy, adding a little of the flour to prevent curdling. Sift the remaining flour with 2 tablespoons of the cocoa powder and fold into the egg mixture. Add a little milk to mix to a soft, dropping consistency.

Beat the remaining sugar in a bowl with the remaining cocoa powder and 250ml/8 fl oz/1 cup hot water. Pour over the mixture in the pie dish. Bake in a preheated oven at 190°C/375°F/gas 5 for about 35 minutes until slightly risen. Dust with icing sugar and serve hot with pouring cream and ice cream.

Cook's Tip

This delicious pudding separates during cooking, giving a spongy topping and a smooth chocolate sauce in the base. Avoid over-cooking as the mixture will dry out.

Chocolate Crêpes with Almonds and Peaches

Serves 4

Crêpes:	100g/3½ oz/1 cup less 2 tablespoons plain (all-purpose) flour
	30ml/2 tablespoons cocoa powder
	1 tablespoon caster (superfine) sugar
	1 egg
	300ml/½ pint/1¼ cups milk
	Oil for frying
Filling:	125g/4 oz white almond paste
	30g/1 oz/¼ cup flaked (slivered) almonds
	4 small ripe peaches, or 8 canned peach halves
Sauce:	150g/5 oz/5 squares plain (dark) chocolate
	150ml/¼ pint/⅔ cup double (heavy) cream

To make the crêpes, sift the flour and cocoa powder into a bowl. Stir in the sugar. Make a well in the centre and add the egg with a little of the milk. Whisk the egg and milk together, incorporating the flour gradually to make a smooth paste. Whisk in the remaining milk to make a batter.

Heat a little oil in a medium frying pan (skillet). Drain off the oil and pour in a little of the batter. Tilt the pan so that the batter coats the entire base of the pan; then cook over a moderate heat until set and golden on underside. Flip the crêpe over with a palette knife and cook until golden. Remove from the pan and add a little more oil. Make seven more crêpes in the same way.

To make the filling, grate the almond paste and toast the almonds lightly. Halve and stone (pit) the peaches.

Arrange a peach half towards one side of a crêpe and sprinkle with about an eighth of the grated almond paste. Fold over the other side of the crêpe to enclose and then roll up into a cone. Place on a large, lightly oiled baking sheet. Fill the remaining crêpes in the same way.

Bake the crêpes in a preheated oven at 180°C/350°F/ gas 4 for about 10 minutes until warmed through. Meanwhile, make the sauce. Break the chocolate into pieces. Bring the cream to the boil in a small saucepan; then stir in the chocolate until it has melted. Transfer the crêpes to serving plates and pour over a little sauce. Serve sprinkled with the toasted nuts.

Cook's Tip

For convenience, the crêpes can be made in advance. Stack between squares of greaseproof paper (baking parchment) to prevent them from sticking together and store in a plastic bag in the refrigerator. They also freeze very well, ready for an easy assembly.

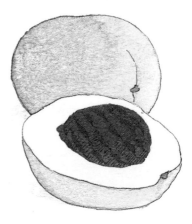

Hot Chocolate Soufflés

Serves 6

90g/3 oz/3 squares plain (dark) chocolate
60g/2 oz/¼ cup unsalted butter
45g/1½ oz/⅓ cup plain (all-purpose) flour
¼ teaspoon ground ginger
300ml/½ pint/1¼ cups milk
5 eggs, separated
30g/1 oz/2½ tablespoons caster (superfine) sugar
Icing (confectioners') sugar for dusting

Grease six individual soufflé dishes. Break the chocolate into pieces. Melt the butter in a large saucepan. Add the flour and ginger and cook, stirring, for 1 minute. Blend in the milk gradually until the mixture is smooth. Bring to the boil and cook, stirring, for 1 minute until thickened. Beat in the chocolate until it has melted. Add the egg yolks.

Whisk the egg whites in a large bowl until stiff. Whisk in the sugar gradually. Using a large metal spoon, fold a quarter of the egg whites into the chocolate mixture; then fold in the remaining egg whites carefully. Turn into the prepared dishes, filling each one almost to the top. Place on a baking sheet and bake in a preheated oven at 190°C/375°F/gas 5 for about 20 minutes until well risen and just firm to the touch. Serve immediately, dusted with icing sugar.

Variations

For additional flavour, add 2 tablespoons brandy or rum, or 2 tablespoons very strong dark coffee when making

Right: Chocolate and Raspberry Torte.

the sauce. If you do not have individual soufflé dishes, use a large 1.4 litre/2½ pint/6 ¼ cup greased dish and allow an extra 20–25 minutes cooking time.

Chocolate and Raspberry Torte

Serves 6

150g/5 oz/⅔ cup unsalted butter, softened
150g/5 oz/generous ¾ cup light muscovado sugar
150g/5 oz/1¼ cups ground almonds
140g/4½ oz/1 cup plus 2 tablespoons self-raising flour
30ml/2 tablespoons cocoa powder
1 egg
225g/8 oz/1½ cups fresh or frozen raspberries
30ml/2 tablespoons flaked (slivered) almonds
Icing (confectioners') sugar for dusting

Grease a 20cm/8 inch spring-release (spring form) cake tin (pan). Beat the butter and sugar together until lightly creamed. Add the ground almonds, flour, cocoa powder and egg, and beat until evenly combined. Press half the mixture into the prepared tin and flatten lightly.

Scatter with the raspberries to within 1cm/½ inch of the edges. Sprinkle with the remaining mixture and top with the almonds. Bake in a preheated oven at 180°C/350°F/gas 4 for 40-50 minutes until slightly risen.

Cool in the tin for 10 minutes; then dust with icing sugar. Serve warm or cold with pouring cream.

Cook's Tip

For a really indulgent pudding, serve with chocolate sauce (p.46).

Creamy Chocolate Rice

Serves 4-5

30g/1 oz/¼ cup chopped mixed nuts
30g/1 oz/2 tablespoons pudding rice
1 tablespoon cocoa powder
1 teaspoon ground mixed spice (apple pie spice)
60g/2 oz/⅓ cup sultanas (golden raisins)
600ml/1 pint/2½ cups milk
150ml/¼ pint/⅔ cup double (heavy) cream
125g/4 oz/4 squares plain (dark) chocolate, roughly chopped
Freshly grated nutmeg for sprinkling

Above: Creamy Chocolate Rice Pudding being prepared.

Grease a 1.15 litre/2 pint/5 cup ovenproof dish lightly. Toast the nuts lightly.

Sprinkle the rice, cocoa powder, spice and sultanas into the dish. Bring the milk and cream to the boil, remove from the heat and stir in the chocolate until it has melted. Pour over the rice mixture, stirring gently. Sprinkle with nutmeg.

Bake in a preheated oven at 150°C/300°F/gas 2 for 1 hour. Stir gently and sprinkle with the nuts. Return to the oven for a further 30–60 minutes until turning golden. Serve hot.

Steamed Chocolate Pudding with Apple and Raisin Topping

Serves 5-6

Topping:
60g/2 oz/¾ cup dried apple chunks, roughly chopped
30g/1 oz/1½ tablespoons dark muscovado sugar
30g/1 oz/3 tablespoons raisins
15g/½ oz/1 tablespoon unsalted butter

Pudding:
90g/3 oz/3 squares plain (dark) or milk chocolate
90g/3 oz/⅓ cup unsalted butter or margarine
90g/3 oz/⅓ cup caster (superfine) sugar
1 egg, separated
60g/2 oz/½ cup self-raising flour
1 teaspoon ground mixed spice (apple pie spice)
1 tablespoon cocoa powder
125g/4 oz/2 cups fresh breadcrumbs
Milk

To make the topping, place the dried apples in a saucepan with the sugar, raisins, butter and 125ml/4 fl oz/ ½ cup water. Bring to the boil, reduce the heat and simmer gently for 10 minutes. Remove from heat and leave to cool.

Butter a 1.15 litre/2 pint/5 cup pudding basin lightly and spoon the apple mixture into the base. To make the pudding, chop the chocolate into small pieces. Cream together the butter or margarine and sugar until pale and creamy. Beat in the egg yolk, then the chopped chocolate. Sift the flour, spice and cocoa powder into the bowl and fold into the mixture with the breadcrumbs. Add enough milk to make a soft dropping consistency.

Whisk the egg white in a separate bowl until stiff, then fold into the chocolate mixture. Spoon into the prepared basin and level the surface. Cover with a double thickness of greaseproof paper (baking parchment) and a layer of foil, securing under the rim. Place in a steamer set over a pan of simmering water. Alternatively, rest on an upturned saucer in a large saucepan. Add enough boiling water to come half-way up the sides of the basin, then cover the pan. Steam for about 2 hours until the pudding feels firm. Invert on a serving plate and serve with pouring cream.

Cook's Tip

Do not forget to check the water level frequently, topping up with boiling water if necessary.

Sticky Blueberry Upside-Down Cake

Serves 4

175g/6 oz/1 cup blueberries
250g/9 oz/9 squares plain (dark) chocolate
125g/4 oz/½ cup unsalted butter
2 eggs
90g/3 oz/½ cup light muscovado sugar
1 teaspoon vanilla essence (extract)
90g/3 oz/¾ cup self-raising flour
45ml/3 tablespoons clear honey or golden (light corn) syrup

Grease and line the base of a 20cm/8 inch round shallow baking tin (pan) or dish. Scatter with the blueberries.

Chop 125g/4 oz/4 squares of the chocolate roughly. Break the remaining chocolate into pieces and place in a heatproof bowl over a pan of simmering water. Add the butter and leave until the mixture has melted. Leave to cool slightly.

Beat together the eggs, sugar and vanilla essence. Beat in the chocolate mixture, then fold in the flour and chopped chocolate. Spoon into the prepared dish and bake in a preheated oven at 190°C/375°F/gas 5 for about 50–60 minutes until firm. Invert on a flat serving dish, peel away the lining paper and drizzle with the honey or syrup. Serve warm with pouring cream or ice cream.

Variation

Substitute 3 small ripe pears for the blueberries. Peel, quarter and core them, and arrange in the base of the dish.

Right: Sticky Blueberry Upside-Down Cake.

Chocolate and Orange Brulées

Serves 4

1 orange
450ml/¾ pint/2 cups double (heavy) cream
175g/6 oz/6 squares plain (dark) chocolate, roughly chopped
4 egg yolks
60g/2 oz/¼ cup caster (superfine) sugar
Icing (confectioners') sugar for dusting

Using a citrus zester, pare strips of rind from the orange. (Alternatively, grate the orange rind.) Place half the rind in a saucepan with the cream and chocolate, and heat gently, stirring until completely smooth.

Place the egg yolks and caster sugar in a bowl and whisk lightly. Pour the chocolate mixture over the yolks gradually, whisking until smooth. Turn into four individual ramekins. Place in a roasting tin (pan) and pour a 1cm/½ inch depth of boiling water into the tin. Cover with foil and bake in a preheated oven at 200°C/400°F/gas 6 for about 15 minutes until beginning to set. Drain off the water.

Sprinkle icing sugar over the ramekins in an even layer. Cook the brulées under a preheated grill (broiler) for several minutes until the sugar begins to caramelize. Scatter with the reserved orange rind and serve dusted with icing sugar.

Variation

Omit the orange rind and add 10ml/2 teaspoons instant coffee granules to the egg yolks with the chocolate.

Next page: Left to right, Chocolate Meringue Pie and Pears with Chocolate and Hazelnuts.

Chocolate Meringue Pie

Serves 6

Pastry:
150g/5 oz/1¼ cups plain (all-purpose) flour
30g/1 oz/¼ cup cocoa powder
90g/3 oz/⅓ cup unsalted butter
2 tablespoons caster (superfine) sugar
1 egg yolk

Filling:
175g/6 oz/6 squares plain (dark) chocolate
90g/3 oz/¾ cup cornflour (cornstarch)
2 egg yolks
60g/2 oz/¼ cup caster (superfine) sugar
600ml/1 pint/2½ cups milk

Meringue:
3 egg whites
175g/6 oz/¾ cup caster (superfine) sugar

To make the pastry, sift the flour and cocoa powder into a bowl. Cut the butter into small pieces, and rub into the flour with your fingertips until the mixture resembles fine breadcrumbs. Stir in the sugar. Add the egg yolk and enough cold water to mix to a firm dough. Transfer to a floured work surface (counter) and knead lightly. Chill for 30 minutes.

Roll out the pastry and use to line a 23cm/9 inch round, loose-based flan tin (pan). Line with greaseproof paper and baking beans and bake in a preheated oven at 200°C/400°F/gas 6 for 15 minutes. Remove the beans and paper.

To make the filling, break the chocolate into pieces. Mix together the cornflour, egg yolks, sugar and a little of the milk. Bring the remaining milk to the boil in a small sauce-pan and pour over the yolk mixture. Return the mixture to the pan, bring to the boil, stirring, and cook until thickened. Remove from the heat and stir in the chocolate until it has melted. Pour into the pastry case and leave to cool.

To make the meringue, whisk the egg whites until stiff. Whisk in the sugar gradually, a little at a time, and whisking well after each addition until the mixture is stiff and glossy. Spoon over the filling and swirl into peaks. Bake for 5 minutes or until the meringue is turning golden. Serve warm with pouring cream.

Cook's Tip

Watch the meringue closely during cooking as it will colour quite suddenly. It looks most appetizing when the tips of the peaks are golden, while some of the meringue remains almost white.

Almond and Chocolate Pithiviers

Serves 6

2 tablespoons flaked (slivered) almonds
60g/2 oz/¼ cup unsalted butter, softened
2 tablespoons brandy

60g/2 oz/½ cup ground almonds
30ml/2 tablespoons cocoa powder
1 egg
60g/2 oz/2 squares plain (dark) chocolate, finely chopped
450g/1 lb puff pastry
Beaten egg for glazing
Icing (confectioners') sugar for dusting

Grease a baking sheet lightly and dampen. Toast the flaked almonds.

Place the butter in a bowl with the brandy and sugar, and beat until light and fluffy. Stir in the ground almonds, cocoa powder, egg and chopped chocolate.

Roll out the pastry on a lightly floured work surface (counter) to a 40x20cm/16x8 inch rectangle. Using a plate as a guide, cut out two circles, each 20cm/8 inches in diameter. Transfer one pastry circle to the prepared baking sheet. Brush the rim of the pastry with water and sprinkle the toasted almonds over the centre. Spoon the almond filling over the toasted almonds, spreading to a flat 'cake' which comes to 5cm/2 inches of the edge of the pastry.

Roll out the remaining pastry circle lightly until slightly larger and lift over the base. Press the edges together to seal. Flute the edges at 2.5cm/1 inch intervals with the back of a knife. Brush the top of the pastry with the beaten egg. Using the tip of a sharp knife, make spiral cuts from the centre of the pastry out to the edges to decorate. Bake in a preheated oven at 200°C/400°F/gas 6 for about 30 minutes until well-risen and deep golden, covering with foil if the pastry starts to over-brown. Dust with icing sugar and serve warm or cold with pouring cream.

Pears with Chocolate and Hazelnuts

Serves 4

4 ripe pears
60g/2 oz/½ cup hazelnuts
90g/3 oz/3 squares plain chocolate
½ teaspoon ground cinnamon
150ml/¼ pint/⅔ cup double (heavy) cream
Icing (confectioners') sugar

Halve the pears and scoop out the cores. Cut a thin slice off each pear so that they sit flat. Place in a large shallow ovenproof dish.

Chop and toast the hazelnuts lightly. Use half to sprinkle into the cavity of each pear. Chop the chocolate roughly and scatter over the pears with the remaining nuts. Sprinkle with the cinnamon. Fill each cavity with a little cream and then dust each pear with icing sugar.

Cook under a preheated moderate grill (broiler) for about 5 minutes until the pears are beginning to colour and the cream is bubbling. Serve hot, with any remaining cream.

Cook's Tip

Choose really ripe, juicy pears which will be easier to cut and much fuller in flavour.

Chocolate Walnut Pie

Serves 8-10

Pastry:
175g/6 oz/1½ cups plain (all-purpose) flour
30g/1 oz/¼ cup cocoa powder
125g/4 oz/½ cup unsalted butter
60g/2 oz/¼ cup caster (superfine) sugar
2 egg yolks

Filling:
175g/6 oz/1 cup light muscovado sugar
150ml/¼ pint/⅔ cup maple syrup
60g/2 oz/¼ cup unsalted butter
½ teaspoon vanilla essence (extract)
2 tablespoons cocoa powder
3 eggs
1 tablespoon milk
225g/8 oz/2 cups broken walnuts

To make the pastry, sift the flour and cocoa powder into a bowl. Cut the butter into small pieces, and rub into the flour with your fingertips until the mixture resembles breadcrumbs. Stir in the sugar and egg yolks with a dash of cold water to make a firm dough. Transfer the dough to a lightly floured surface and knead lightly. Chill for 30 minutes. Roll out the pastry and use to line a 23cm/9 inch loose-based flan tin (pan).

To make the filling, place the sugar and syrup in a saucepan and heat gently until the sugar has dissolved. Pour into a bowl and stir in the butter and vanilla essence. Add the cocoa powder, eggs and milk, and beat until smooth. Sprinkle half the walnuts into the pastry case and

Right: Chocolate Walnut Pie.

42

pour over the syrup mixture. Sprinkle with the remaining nuts. Bake in a preheated oven at 200°C/400°F/gas 6 for 10 minutes, then reduce the oven temperature to 170°C/325°F/gas 3 and bake for a further 40–45 minutes until just set. Serve warm or cold with pouring cream.

Cook's Tip

Keep an eye on the pie towards the end of cooking time. Cover it with foil if it starts to overbrown.

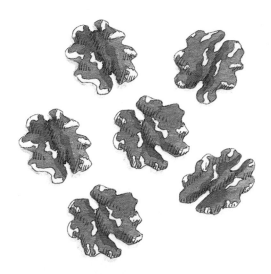

A special chocolate dessert provides the perfect excuse for combining all our favourite ingredients in one delicious concoction! Chocolate, cream and liqueurs are the basis of delicious desserts such as the Chocolate Truffle Slice (p.56), Layered Chocolate Trifle (p.48) or White Chocolate Creams (p.47). There are also classic recipes in this chapter like Profiteroles (this page) with a Glossy Chocolate Sauce and interesting variations on a Pavlova (p.54) and White Chocolate Roulade (p.58).

Although these recipes require a little time for preparation, most can be made a day in advance, for finishing with cream and other decorations an hour before serving.

Previous page: Left to right, White Chocolate Creams, Profiteroles with Glossy Chocolate Sauce and Layered Chocolate Trifle.

Profiteroles with Glossy Chocolate Sauce

Serves 5-6

Pastry: 75g/2½ oz/¼ cup plus 2 tablespoons plain (all-purpose) flour
60g/2 oz/¼ cup unsalted butter
2 eggs, lightly beaten

Sauce: 150g/5 oz/5 squares plain (dark) chocolate
15g/½ oz/1 tablespoon unsalted butter
2 tablespoons golden (light corn) syrup

To Finish: 150ml/¼ pint/⅔ cup double (heavy) cream
1 tablespoon icing (confectioners') sugar
Extra icing sugar for dusting

Grease 2 baking sheets lightly and dampen. Sift the flour on to a plate or piece of paper.

Place the butter in a small saucepan with 150ml/¼ pint/⅔ cup water. Heat gently until the butter melts; then bring to the boil. Remove from the heat immediately and add the sifted flour. Beat thoroughly until smooth. Return to the heat and cook until the mixture comes away cleanly from the sides of the pan. Leave to cool for 2 minutes.

Beat in the eggs, a little at a time, until the mixture is smooth and glossy. Place in a piping bag fitted with a large plain tube (tip). Pipe small blobs, about 2.5cm/1 inch in diameter, on to the baking sheets. Bake in a preheated oven at 220°C/425°F/gas 7 for 20 minutes until well-risen, crisp and golden. Remove from the oven and make a cut in the side of each bun. Return to the oven for a further 5 minutes for the centres to dry out. Transfer to a wire rack to cool.

To make the sauce, break the chocolate into pieces and place in a saucepan with the butter, syrup and 1 tablespoon cold water. Heat gently, stirring until smooth and glossy.

Whip the cream with the icing sugar until it is just peaking. Spoon or pipe into the choux buns and pile up on a serving plate. Dust with icing sugar and pour over a little chocolate sauce. Serve any remaining sauce separately.

Variation

For a special dessert, add a splash of brandy or orange-favoured liqueur to the cream when whipping.

White Chocolate Creams

Serves 6

2 small ripe bananas
1 tablespoon lemon juice
175g/6 oz/6 squares white chocolate
300ml/½ pint/1¼ cups milk
300ml/½ pint/1¼ cups double (heavy) cream
4 egg yolks
30g/1 oz/3 tablespoons caster (superfine) sugar
1 teaspoon cornflour (cornstarch)
2 tablespoons Cointreau or orange-flavoured liqueur

To Decorate: 90g/3 oz/3 squares plain (dark) or milk chocolate
2 tablespoons double (heavy) cream
Fresh mint leaves
Chocolate mint leaves (p.6), optional
Icing (confectioners') sugar for dusting

Peel the bananas and slice thinly. Toss with the lemon juice and spoon into six tall stemmed glasses. Break the chocolate into small pieces.

Put the milk and cream into a saucepan and heat gently. Beat together the egg yolks, sugar and cornflour in a bowl.

Pour the hot milk and cream over the egg yolk mixture, stirring. Return to the saucepan and cook gently until thick enough to coat the back of a wooden spoon. Remove from the heat and stir in the white chocolate until it has melted; then add the liqueur. Leave to cool slightly; then spoon over the bananas in the glasses. Leave to cool completely.

To decorate, break the chocolate into pieces and melt with the cream in a heatproof bowl over a pan of simmering water. Spoon over the desserts, swirling to the edges of the glasses. Decorate with fresh mint leaves and chocolate mint leaves, if liked. Dust lightly with icing sugar.

Variation

Use plain or milk chocolate instead of the white chocolate, and add 2 teaspoons cocoa powder. White or dark rum can be added instead of the orange-flavoured liqueur.

Rich Chocolate Bavarois

Serves 6

225g/8 oz/8 squares plain (dark) chocolate
15g/½ oz/1 envelope powdered gelatine
3 egg yolks
45g/1½ oz/3 tablespoons caster (superfine) sugar
1 teaspoon cornflour (cornstarch)
300ml/½ pint/1¼ cups milk
1 egg white
300ml/½ pint/1¼ cups double (heavy) cream

To Serve:

Raspberries
Redcurrants
Blackcurrants
Mint leaves
Icing (confectioners') sugar for dusting

Break the chocolate into pieces. Sprinkle the gelatine over 3 tablespoons water in a small bowl. Whisk the egg yolks with 15g/½ oz/1 tablespoon of the sugar and the cornflour. Bring the milk to the boil in a saucepan and pour over the egg yolk mixture, stirring. Return the mixture to the pan and heat gently, stirring continuously until slightly thickened. Remove from the heat and stir in the gelatine, then the chocolate until smooth. Leave the custard to cool.

Whisk the egg white until stiff; then whisk in the remaining sugar gradually. Whip the cream until it is just peaking. Using a large metal spoon, fold the cream into the chocolate mixture carefully; then fold in the egg white. Spoon into a wetted 1.15 litre/2 pint/5 cup jelly mould or six individual moulds and chill until just set.

To serve the bavarois, dip the mould into a bowl of very hot water for several seconds and then invert on a serving plate, shaking the mould to release the bavarois. Surround with raspberries, redcurrants and blackcurrants and decorate with mint leaves. Dust the fruits with icing sugar.

Cook's Tip

Dip the mould very cautiously when releasing the bavarois, returning the mould to the water in short bursts if necessary. If the mould is steeped for too long, the edges of the bavarois will melt and look very messy.

Layered Chocolate Trifle

Serves 6-8

225g/8 oz almond macaroon biscuits (cookies)
350g/12 oz ripe apricots
3 tablespoons Tia Maria or brandy
90g/3 oz/3 squares plain (dark) chocolate
1 egg yolk
2 teaspoons cornflour (cornstarch)
1 tablespoon caster (superfine) sugar
300ml/½ pint/1¼ cups milk

Topping:

3 tablespoons Tia Maria
3 tablespoons strong dark coffee
60ml/4 tablespoons icing (confectioners') sugar
300ml/½ pint/1¼ cups double (heavy) cream
Cocoa powder for dusting
Piped chocolate pieces to decorate (p.7)

Place the biscuits in a glass serving dish. Halve and remove the stones (pits) from the apricots. Cut them into wedges and scatter over the biscuits. Spoon over the liqueur or brandy.

Break the chocolate into pieces. Mix the egg yolk,

cornflour, sugar and a dash of the milk in a bowl. Bring the remaining milk to the boil and pour over the egg yolk mixture, whisking well; then return it to the saucepan. Cook, stirring, until thickened. Remove from the heat and stir in the chocolate until it has melted. Leave to cool, then pour the custard over the apricots and level the surface. Leave to cool completely.

To make the topping, place the Tia Maria, coffee, icing sugar and cream in a bowl and whip until the mixture forms soft peaks. Spoon over the chocolate custard. Dust lightly with cocoa powder and finish with piped chocolate decorations.

Cook's Tip

Make sure the apricots are the soft, dessert variety. If preferred, used canned apricots, or substitute a mixture of soft fruits.

Petit Pots au Chocolat

Serves 6	225g/8 oz/8 squares plain (dark) chocolate
	300ml/½ pint/1¼ cups milk
	300ml/½ pint/1¼ cups single (light) cream
	1 teaspoon vanilla essence (extract)
	1 egg
	3 egg yolks
	30g/1 oz/2½ tablespoons caster (superfine) sugar
To Decorate:	Whipped cream
	Cocoa powder for dusting

Break the chocolate into pieces. Place the milk, cream and vanilla essence in a saucepan and bring just to the boil. Stir in the chocolate until it has melted.

Mix together the egg, egg yolks and sugar in a large bowl. Beat in the chocolate mixture. Strain into six small ramekins or small ovenproof cups. Stand the containers in a roasting tin (pan), then pour a 2cm/¾ inch depth of water into the tin. Cover with foil and bake in a preheated oven at 150°C/300°F/gas 2 for 50–60 minutes until the custard feels lightly set. Remove from the oven and leave to cool, then chill until ready to serve. Top each serving with lightly whipped cream and dust with cocoa powder.

Variation

For a mildly spiced flavour, add ½ teaspoon ground cinnamon when mixing the eggs. Alternatively, try adding the finely grated rind of ½ orange.

Next page: Left to right, Petit Pots au Chocolat and Rich Chocolate Bavarois.

Chocolate Swirled Cheesecake

Serves 10-12

Base:
175g/6 oz digestive biscuits (graham crackers)
90g/3 oz/⅓ cup unsalted butter
30g/1 oz/2 tablespoons light muscovado sugar

Filling:
125g/4 oz/4 squares plain (dark) chocolate
500g/1 lb 2 oz/2¼ cups cream cheese
90g/3 oz/½ cup light muscovado sugar
15g/½ oz/2 tablespoons plain (all-purpose) flour
3 eggs
2 tablespoons cocoa powder
30g/1 oz/3 tablespoons raisins
1 teaspoon vanilla essence (extract)

Grease and line a 20cm/8 inch spring-release (spring form) cake tin (pan). Place the biscuits in a thick plastic bag and crush with a rolling pin. Melt the butter in a saucepan. Add the crushed biscuits and sugar, and stir until evenly combined. Spoon into the prepared tin and spread evenly over the base. Pack down lightly with the back of the spoon.

To make the filling, break the chocolate into pieces and melt in a heatproof bowl over a saucepan of simmering water. Put the cream cheese in a bowl and beat with the sugar until smooth. Beat in the flour and eggs. Spoon a third of the mixture into a separate bowl and beat in the melted chocolate and cocoa powder. Beat the raisins and vanilla essence into the plain mixture.

Place alternate spoonfuls of the chocolate and vanilla-flavoured mixture in the tin. Using a skewer, swirl the two mixtures together lightly to give a marbled effect. Bake in a preheated oven at 160°C/325°F/gas 3 for about 1 hour, then turn off the oven and leave the cheesecake to cool slightly in the oven for a further 1 hour. Serve warm or chilled with pouring cream.

Cook's Tip

This delicious cheesecake is very rich, so serve small portions. If preferred, substitute roughly chopped, toasted hazelnuts or walnuts for the raisins.

Chocolate Coconut Torte

Serves 10-12

Filling:
400g/14 oz/14 squares white chocolate
2 eggs, separated
750ml/1¼ pints/3 cups double (heavy) cream
125g/4 oz/4 squares plain (dark) chocolate
3 tablespoons Cointreau or orange-flavoured liqueur

Base:
225g/8oz coconut biscuits (cookies)
125g/4 oz/½ cup unsalted butter

Grease the base and sides of a 23cm/9 inch round loose-based cake tin (pan). Line with greaseproof paper (baking parchment), but do not grease the paper.

Break the white chocolate into pieces and melt in a heatproof bowl with the egg yolks and 4 tablespoons of the cream. Melt the plain chocolate in a separate bowl with the liqueur. Whip 150ml/¼ pint/⅔ cup of the cream lightly and mix with the plain chocolate. Place in a piping bag fitted with a 1cm/½ inch plain tube (tip) and pipe dots, about 2cm/¾ inch in diameter, on to the base of the prepared tin. Reserve the remainder and chill the tin.

Whip the remaining cream and fold in the white chocolate mixture. Spoon over the dark chocolate in the tin and level the surface. Pipe the remaining dark chocolate in the bag immediately into the white chocolate, to create spots of colour when the torte is sliced.

To make the base, place the biscuits in a strong plastic bag and crush finely with a rolling pin. Melt the butter in a saucepan and stir in the crushed biscuits until evenly coated. Scatter over the chocolate mixture in the tin and press down lightly. Chill for several hours or overnight.

To serve, invert the torte on a serving plate and peel away the lining paper. Serve very small slices.

Cook's Tip

Both chocolate mixtures set firm quite soon so you will need to work quickly when assembling the torte. It will help slightly to use the cream at room temperature.

Mud Pie

Serves 8

Pastry:
175g/6 oz/1½ cups plain (all-purpose) flour
125g/4 oz/½ cup unsalted butter
30g/1 oz/2 tablespoons light muscovado sugar
2 teaspoons instant coffee powder

Filling:
1½ teaspoons powdered gelatine
200g/7 oz/7 squares plain (dark) chocolate
90g/3 oz/½ cup light muscovado sugar
2 tablespoons cornflour (cornstarch)
2 egg yolks
300ml/½ pint/1¼ cups milk
1 tablespoon instant coffee powder
450ml/¾ pint/2 cups double (heavy) cream
Grated chocolate or chocolate chips to decorate
Cocoa powder for dusting

To make the pastry, sift the flour into a bowl. Cut the butter into small pieces, and rub into the flour with your fingertips until the mixture begins to bind together. Stir in the sugar and coffee powder, and mix to a dough.

Grease a 20cm/8 inch loose-based flan tin (pan) lightly. Press the pastry dough around the base and sides of the tin until evenly lined. Bake in a preheated oven at 180°C/ 350°F/gas 4 for 20 minutes; then leave to cool.

To make the filling, sprinkle the gelatine over 2 tablespoons water in a small bowl. Leave to soften. Break the chocolate into pieces. Beat the sugar, cornflour and egg yolks together. Place the milk in a saucepan with the coffee powder. Bring just to the boil; then pour over the egg yolk mixture. Return to the saucepan and cook, stirring, until thickened. Stir in the softened gelatine. When it has dissolved, add the chocolate and stir until smooth and melted. Stir in 300ml/½ pint/1¼ cups of the cream and pour into the prepared case. Cover and chill until lightly set.

Whip the remaining cream very lightly and swirl over the filling. Decorate with grated chocolate or chocolate chips and serve dusted with cocoa powder.

Cook's Tip

The rich, gooey filling of this delicious pie will have a slightly firmer texture if left to set overnight. For a lighter, more everyday version, use a shortcrust (plain) pastry case and replace the cream in the filling with additional milk.

Chocolate Chip Pavlova

Serves 8-10

5 egg whites
300g/11 oz/scant 1½ cups caster (superfine) sugar
90g/3 oz/¾ cup plain (dark) or milk chocolate chips
2 teaspoons white wine vinegar
2 teaspoons cornflour (cornstarch)

To Decorate:

225g/8 oz/1½ cups strawberries
125g/4 oz/4 squares plain (dark) chocolate
300ml/½ pint/1¼ cups double (heavy) cream
1 tablespoon icing (confectioners') sugar

Grease a large baking sheet lightly and line with non-stick baking parchment. Draw a 21cm/8½ inch circle on the paper, using a plate as a guide.

Right: Chocolate Chip Pavlova.

Place the egg whites in a large, clean bowl and whisk until stiff. Whisk in the caster sugar gradually, a tablespoonful at a time, until the mixture is very thick and glossy, ensuring that the mixture is whisked well between each addition. Fold in the chocolate chips lightly, then the vinegar and cornflour.

Spoon the meringue on to the prepared baking sheet and spread to the edge of the marked circle, swirling the mixture attractively into soft peaks. Bake in a preheated oven at 150°C/300°F/gas 2 for 5 minutes, then reduce the oven temperature to 120°C/250°F/gas ½ and bake for a further 1 hour or until the meringue is crisp. Leave to cool on the baking sheet.

To decorate, dip the strawberries in 60g/2 oz/2 squares of the melted chocolate (p.71). Use the remaining chocolate to make chocolate rose leaves (p.6).

Whip the cream with the icing sugar until it is peaking. Transfer the meringue to a serving plate and swirl with the cream. Scatter the dipped strawberries over the surface and decorate with the chocolate leaves.

Chocolate Truffle Slice

Serves 10-12

90g/3 oz ginger snap biscuits (cookies)
Piece of stem (candied) ginger,
plus 4 tablespoons of juices from the jar
450g/1 lb plain (dark) chocolate
60g/2 oz/¼ cup unsalted butter
600ml/1 pint/2½ cups double (heavy) cream
4 tablespoons brandy

To Finish:

Crushed biscuits
Cocoa powder
Icing (confectioners') sugar

Put the biscuits in a strong plastic bag and crush firmly with a rolling pin. Grease and line the sides only of a 23cm/9 inch spring-release (spring form) tin (pan) and scatter the biscuits over the base.

Chop the stem ginger finely. Break the chocolate into pieces and place in a heavy-based saucepan with the butter, chopped ginger and the juices. Cook over a very gentle heat until the butter and chocolate have melted. Stir until smooth.

Whip the cream with the brandy until it begins to thicken. Place the chocolate mixture in a separate bowl and fold in the cream gradually until evenly combined. Spoon over the biscuits in the tin and level the surface. Cover and chill for several hours or overnight.

To serve, transfer the cake to a serving plate and peel away the lining paper. Dust generously with crushed biscuits, icing sugar and cocoa powder, and serve in small slices.

Chocolate Mousse Cups

Serves 6

Cups: 225g/8 oz/8 squares plain (dark) chocolate
1 small orange

Mousse: 125g/4 oz/4 squares plain (dark) chocolate
4 eggs, separated

To Decorate: Small selection of fresh fruits, such as
strawberries, redcurrants, raspberries, kiwi fruit and grapes

To make the cups, break the chocolate into pieces and melt in a heatproof bowl over a saucepan of simmering water. Cut a double-thickness circle of foil, about 18cm/7 inches in diameter, and wrap around a whole orange, letting the edges open out slightly to make a cup shape. Remove from the orange and press the foil case on to the work surface (counter) to make a flat base. Make five more cases in the same way.

Spoon a little of the melted chocolate into one of the foil cases. Smooth up the sides with the back of a teaspoon, giving the edges an uneven, rough edge. Repeat on the remaining cups. Chill the cups until set firmly. Peel away the foil from each cup carefully, starting around the top edges, and peeling down to the base. Place the cases on a small tray on baking sheet.

To make the mousse, break the chocolate into pieces and melt with 2 tablespoons boiling water in a heatproof bowl over a saucepan of simmering water. Add the yolks to the melted chocolate and stir gently. Whisk the egg whites in a

Left: Chocolate Truffle Slice.

large bowl until stiff. Using a large metal spoon, fold a quarter into the chocolate mixture; then fold in the remainder carefully.

Spoon the mousse into the chocolate cases and leave for several hours until set. Arrange the fruits over the cases to decorate before serving.

Cook's Tip

The mousse filling is one of the simplest and most delicious you can make. Serve it in small glasses with a swirl of cream as a quick and easy dessert.

White Chocolate Roulade

Serves 8

Roulade: 150g/5 oz/5 squares white chocolate
4 eggs, separated
90g/3 oz/⅓ cup caster (superfine) sugar
Extra caster (superfine) sugar for sprinkling

To Finish: 450g/1 lb soft fruits such as strawberries,
raspberries, blackcurrants and redcurrants
75ml/2½ fl oz/5 tablespoons kirsch
2 tablespoons caster (superfine) sugar
150ml/¼ pint/⅔ cup crème fraiche

Grease and line a 33x23cm/13x9 inch Swiss (jelly) roll tin (pan) with greased non-stick baking parchment. Break the chocolate into pieces and melt in a heatproof bowl over a saucepan of simmering water.

Whisk the egg yolks in a bowl with the sugar. Beat in the melted chocolate and 1 tablespoon hot water. Whisk the egg whites until stiff. Using a large metal spoon, fold a

quarter of the egg whites carefully into the chocolate mixture; then fold in the remainder. Spoon into the prepared tin and ease the mixture gently into the corners. Bake in a preheated oven at 180°C/350°F/gas 4 for 20-25 minutes until risen and just firm to the touch.

Sprinkle a clean sheet of non-stick baking parchment with caster sugar. Invert the cake on the paper and peel away the lining paper. Cover with a damp tea-towel (dish cloth) and leave to cool.

Halve any large strawberries and mix in a bowl with 4 tablespoons of the kirsch and 1 tablespoon of the sugar. Leave until ready to serve, stirring occasionally.

Stir the remaining kirsch and sugar into the crème fraîche and spread over the roulade. Roll up the roulade starting from a short end, pulling up the paper underneath to help it to roll easily. Transfer to a serving plate and dust with a little extra sugar. Transfer the fruits to a serving bowl. Serve the roulade with spoonfuls of fruit.

Cook's Tip

Crème fraîche makes a lovely contrast with the sweetness of the chocolate. Lightly whipped double (heavy) cream can be used instead if preferred.

Left: White Chocolate Roulade served with soft fruits.

Rich in cream and real chocolate, there is nothing to beat the delicious flavour of home-made ice cream. Using whisked eggs and cream, the following recipes are simple to follow and can, of course, be made two to three weeks in advance.

For special occasion desserts there are some frozen gâteaus like the Chocolate Cherry Meringue (p.67), White Chocolate and Coffee Torte (p.62) and Chocolate Macaroon Tortoni (p.66). All these ease the burden of last-minute preparation, and simply need to be transferred to the refrigerator for a short time before serving to make slicing or scooping easier.

Iced Chocolate Mousse

Serves 6

150g/5 oz/5 squares plain (dark) chocolate
60g/2 oz/½ cup cocoa powder
2 tablespoons golden (light corn) syrup
2 tablespoons brandy
4 eggs
2 egg yolks
150ml/¼ pint/⅔ cup double (heavy) cream
Feathered chocolate pieces (p.7) to decorate

Break the chocolate into pieces and melt in a heatproof bowl over a saucepan of simmering water. Add the cocoa powder, golden syrup and brandy, and stir until smooth.

Place the eggs and extra egg yolks in a large bowl and whisk with an electric whisk until thick and pale. Whip the cream in a separate bowl until it is just peaking.

Pour the chocolate mixture over the whisked eggs, then fold in gently using a large metal spoon. Fold in the cream. Spoon the mixture into a freezer container and freeze overnight until firm.

Using an ice cream scoop, take small balls of the ice cream and arrange in serving glasses. Serve decorated with feathered chocolate pieces.

Variation
For a dinner party dessert, serve the iced chocolate mousse in pretty chocolate cases (p.57).

Opposite: Top, Iced Chocolate Mousse, bottom, Chocolate Macaroon Tortoni (p.66).

White Chocolate and Coffee Torte

Serves 8-10	300ml/½ pint/1¼ cups strong black coffee
	4 tablespoons Tia Maria or Kahlua
	350g/12 oz/12 squares white chocolate
	600ml/1 pint/2½ cups double (heavy) cream
	60g/2 oz/½ cup chocolate coffee beans
	1 tablespoon icing (confectioners') sugar
	2 packets sponge fingers (lady-fingers)
To Decorate:	Run-out chocolate leaves (p.7)
	Extra chocolate coffee beans
	Cocoa powder for dusting

Mix the coffee with the Tia Maria or Kahlua in a bowl. Break the chocolate into pieces and place in a heavy-based saucepan with 300ml/½ pint/1¼ cups of the cream. Cook very gently, stirring frequently until the chocolate has melted and the mixture is smooth. Remove from the heat and pour into a bowl. Stir in the remaining cream and leave to cool.

Place the chocolate coffee beans in a strong plastic bag and crush with a rolling pin until fairly finely ground. Dip the sponge fingers briefly in the coffee liquid so that a little is absorbed but the biscuits do not turn soggy. Transfer to a plate. When all the biscuits have been dipped, add any remaining liquid to the cream and whip until mixture is softly peaking.

Spoon a third of the cream into the base of a 23cm/ 9 inch round spring-release (spring form) tin (pan). Arrange half the sponge fingers over the cream, so that they are evenly layered. Scatter half the chocolate coffee beans on top. Spread half the remaining cream over the

sponge fingers and then cover with the remaining sponge fingers. Scatter the remaining coffee beans on top. Spoon the remaining cream into the tin and spread to the edges, swirling the surface attractively. Cover the tin and freeze overnight.

To serve, loosen the edges of the tin with a knife and then remove the sides of the tin. Slide a fish slice under the cake and transfer to a flat serving plate. Chill for 1–2 hours before serving partially frozen, or leave to thaw completely. Decorate with the chocolate leaves and coffee beans, and serve dusted with cocoa powder.

Cook's Tip

Chocolate coffee beans are available from some confectioners and delicatessens. If you cannot find any, substitute the same quantity of plain (dark) chocolate, finely chopped.

Left: White Chocolate and Coffee Torte.

Chunky Chocolate Fudge Ice Cream

Serves 6-8	175g/6 oz/6 squares plain (dark) chocolate
	90g/3 oz creamy fudge
	6 eggs, separated
	125g/4 oz/½ cups caster (superfine) sugar
	300ml/½ pint/1¼ cups double (heavy) cream
To Serve:	30g/1 oz/¼ cup broken walnuts or pecan nuts, toasted
	Dessert biscuits (cookies)

Break the chocolate into pieces and melt in a heatproof bowl over a saucepan of simmering water. Cut the fudge into small chunks.

Whisk the egg whites in a large bowl until stiff. Whisk in the sugar gradually, a teaspoonful at a time, until the mixture is stiff and glossy.

Whisk the egg yolks in a separate bowl, until pale. Beat in the melted chocolate gradually. Whip the cream until it is just peaking; then fold it into the egg yolk mixture with the chunks of fudge. Using a large metal spoon; fold a quarter of the egg white into the chocolate mixture to lighten it; then fold in the remainder carefully. Spoon into a freezer container and freeze overnight until firm.

To serve, scoop the ice cream into glass serving dishes and scatter with toasted nuts. Serve with dessert biscuits.

Cook's Tip

This makes an ice cream with a really creamy texture, perfect for serving straight from the freezer. If liked, serve with a rich chocolate sauce like the one on page 31.

Chocolate Ripple Ice

Serves 4

90g/3 oz/3 squares plain (dark) chocolate
250g/9 oz/generous 1 cup mascarpone cheese
2 eggs, separated
30g/1 oz/2 tablespoons caster (superfine) sugar
1 teaspoon vanilla essence (extract)
Dessert biscuits (cookies) to serve

Break the chocolate into pieces and melt in a heatproof bowl over a saucepan of simmering water.

Beat the mascarpone cheese in a bowl with the egg yolks and sugar until very smooth and creamy. Spoon half the mixture into a separate bowl and beat in the melted chocolate. Beat the vanilla into the remaining mixture.

Whisk the egg whites in a separate bowl until stiff. Using a metal spoon, fold half the egg white into the chocolate mixture and half into the vanilla mixture. Alternate spoonfuls of the two mixtures into a freezer container. Using a metal skewer, swirl the two mixtures together roughly. Freeze overnight until firm.

To serve, leave the ice cream at room temperature for 15 minutes; then scoop into serving glasses. Serve with dessert biscuits.

Left: A selection of frozen delights, left to right, Chunky Chocolate Fudge Ice Cream, Chocolate Ripple Ice and Chocolate Sorbet.

Chocolate Macaroon Tortoni

Serves 8

175g/6 oz/1½ cups no-need-to-soak prunes, roughly chopped
2 tablespoons brandy
175g/6 oz/6 squares plain (dark) chocolate
450ml/¾ pint/2 cups double (heavy) cream
30g/1 oz/3 tablespoons icing (confectioners') sugar
225g/8 oz macaroon or ameretti biscuits (cookies)
White chocolate rose leaves (p.6) to decorate

Place the prunes in a bowl with the brandy. Cover and leave to soak while preparing the ice cream.

Break the chocolate into pieces and place in a heatproof bowl over a saucepan of simmering water. Add 150ml/¼ pint/⅔ cup of the cream and leave until melted. Remove from the heat and stir until smooth.

Whip the remaining cream lightly in a bowl with the icing sugar. Stir in the melted chocolate mixture. Spoon into a freezer container and freeze for 2–3 hours until partially frozen.

Place the biscuits in a thick plastic bag and beat with a rolling pin until finely crushed. Remove the ice cream from the freezer and mash lightly until broken up. Stir in half the crushed biscuits.

Spoon a third of the mixture into a 900g/2 lb loaf tin (pan) and scatter with half the prune mixture. Cover with half the remaining ice cream and then the remaining prune mixture. Finally cover with the remaining ice cream mixture and level the surface. Return to the freezer for several hours or overnight until firm.

Dip the tin briefly into hot water; then invert the ice cream on a serving plate. Press the reserved biscuits around the sides. Decorate with chocolate leaves and serve cut into slices.

Variation

Use no-need-to-soak dried apricots or dates instead of the prunes. Ginger wine or sherry can be used instead of the brandy.

Chocolate Cherry Meringue

Serves 10

Meringue:

4 egg whites

225g/8 oz/1 cup caster (superfine) sugar

90g/3 oz/½ cup plain (dark) or milk chocolate chips

Filling and Decoration:

2x400g/14 oz can stoned (pitted) black cherries, drained

3 tablespoons kirsch

600ml/1 pint/2½ cups double (heavy) cream

30g/1 oz/3 tablespoons icing (confectioners') sugar

125g/4 oz/4 squares milk chocolate, finely grated

60g/2 oz/2 squares plain (dark) chocolate

Small bunch of fresh cherries

Draw three 23cm/9 inch circles on non-stick baking parchment, using a plate as a guide. Place on three baking sheets.

To make the meringue, whisk the egg whites until stiff. Whisk in the sugar gradually, a tablespoonful at a time, whisking well after each addition, until the mixture is stiff and glossy. Fold in the chocolate chips. Divide the mixture between the three circles, spreading to the edges with a palette knife. Bake in a preheated oven at 150°C/275°F/gas 1 for about 1 hour until crisp, rotating the baking sheets on the shelves half-way through cooking. Remove from the oven, peel off the lining paper and leave to cool.

Chop the canned cherries roughly and mix with the kirsch. Whip the cream with the icing sugar and grated milk chocolate until it is only just holding its shape.

Place a meringue layer on a baking sheet or freezer-proof serving plate. Spread with a little of the cream and scatter half the cherries on top. Cover with another meringue layer and a little more cream. Scatter the remaining cherries on top. Cover with the remaining meringue layer. Using a palette knife; spread the remaining cream over the top and sides of the gâteau, smoothing it down as evenly as possible. Open-freeze until firm.

To serve, remove the meringue from freezer and transfer to a flat serving plate if frozen on a baking sheet. Use the plain chocolate and fresh cherries to make dipped fruits (p.7). Leave the meringue to thaw at room temperature for at least 1 hour; then serve decorated with the dipped cherries.

Chocolate Fruit Bombes

Serves 6

Ice Cream:
150g/5 oz/5 squares plain (dark) chocolate
300ml/½ pint/1¼ cups milk
3 egg yolks
1 teaspoon vanilla essence (extract)
2 teaspoons cornflour (cornstarch)
60g/2 oz/¼ cup caster (superfine) sugar
300ml/½ pint/1¼ cups double (heavy) cream

To Finish:
600ml/1 pint/2½ cups good quality bought sorbet
such as mango, orange, strawberry or another soft fruit
90g/3 oz/3 squares plain (dark) or milk chocolate
15g/½ oz/1 tablespoon butter
Appropriate fruits to decorate
Sprigs of fresh mint

To make the ice cream, break the chocolate into pieces and place in a saucepan with the milk. Heat gently until the chocolate melts. Bring to the boil, then remove from the heat and leave to cool slightly. Beat the egg yolks, vanilla essence, cornflour and sugar together until creamy. Blend in the chocolate mixture gradually. Strain the mixture back into the saucepan and cook over a gentle heat, stirring continuously until slightly thickened. Remove from the heat and pour into a bowl. Leave to cool completely.

Whisk the cream gradually into the cooled custard, then spoon into a freezer container and freeze overnight until firm.

Place six individual pudding moulds in the freezer to chill. Remove the ice cream from the freezer and leave at room temperature for 20–30 minutes until softened enough

to scoop. Spread the softened ice cream around the base and sides of the moulds in an even layer, leaving a large cavity in the centre. Return to the freezer for at least 1 hour or until firm.

Leave the sorbet at room temperature until slightly softened; then pack it into the centre of each mould, making sure that the surface of each one is level. Return to the freezer for a further 1 hour or until firm.

To decorate the ice cream bombes, dip each mould very briefly in hot water until just loosened; then tap out on to serving plates. Return to the freezer while melting the chocolate.

Break up the chocolate and melt in a heatproof bowl with the butter over a saucepan of simmering water. Place in a piping bag fitted with a writing tube (tip). (Alternatively, use a paper piping bag and snip off the tip.) Drizzle random lines of chocolate over the ice cream. Serve decorated with fresh fruits and sprigs of mint.

Cook's Tip

Although these prettily moulded ice creams take a little while to prepare, they can be made several days in advance. Even the chocolate can be piped into the unmoulded ice cream and returned to the freezer in a rigid container. Leave the bombes at room temperature for 10 minutes before serving.

Left: Chocolate Fruit Bombes.

Chocolate Sorbet

Serves 6

1 teaspoon powdered gelatine
175g/6 oz/¾ cup granulated sugar
200g/7 oz/7 squares plain (dark) chocolate
150ml/¼ pint/⅔ cup single (light) cream
2 egg yolks
1 teaspoon vanilla essence (extract)
Mint leaves to decorate

Sprinkle the gelatine over 2 tablespoons water in a small bowl. Leave to soften. Place the sugar in a heavy-based saucepan with 600ml/1 pint/2½ cups water. Heat gently, stirring, until the sugar has completely dissolved. Bring to the boil and boil for 5 minutes until it is syrupy. Remove from the heat and cool for 3 minutes. Stir in the gelatine until dissolved; then leave to cool completely.

Break the chocolate into pieces and place in a heatproof bowl with the cream, egg yolks and vanilla essence. Rest the bowl over a pan of simmering water and leave until the chocolate has melted. Stir the mixture frequently until it is completely smooth. Remove from the heat and pour in the sugar syrup, stirring well.

Scoop the mixture into a freezer container and freeze for 2–3 hours until partially frozen. Remove from the freezer and mash lightly. Beat with an electric whisk until smooth. Re-freeze the sorbet until completely firm. Serve scooped into glasses, decorated with mint leaves.

Cook's Tip

If you have the time, re-freeze the whisked sorbet partially for a second time and then whisk once again before freezing until firm. This will give an even smoother result.

INDEX

After Dinner Mints	10
Bavarois, Rich Chocolate	48
Brulées, Chocolate and Orange	37
Cheesecake, Chocolate Swirled	52
Cherries, Brandied Chocolate	11
Coconut Kisses	19
Colettes, Chocolate	22
Crêpes with Almonds and Peaches, Chocolate	31
Decorative ideas	6-7
Easter Eggs, Decorating	27
Easter Eggs, Home-made	26
Easter Eggs, Wrapping	27
Fruit Bombes, Chocolate	68
Fruits, Double-Dipped	17
Fudge, Chocolate Walnut	23
Fudge, Chocolate-Dipped	14
Ice Cream, Chunky Chocolate Fudge	64
Layer Pudding, Chocolate	30
Lollies, Chocolate	13
Macaroon Tortoni, Chocolate	66
Marzipan, Chequered Chocolate	18
Meringue Pie, Chocolate	40
Meringue, Chocolate Cherry	67
Mice, Chocolate	12
Mousse Cups, Chocolate	57
Mousse, Iced Chocolate	60
Mud Pie	53
Orange Logs, Chocolate	16
Pavlova, Chocolate Chip	54
Peanut Brittle, Chocolate-Coated	20
Pears with Chocolate and Hazelnuts	41
Petit Pots au Chocolat	49
Pithiviers, Almond and Chocolate	41
Praline Squares, Chocolate	11
Profiteroles with Glossy Chocolate Sauce	46
Rice, Creamy Chocolate	34
Ripple Ice, Chocolate	65
Rocky Roads	21
Roulade, White Chocolate	58
Sorbet, Chocolate	70
Soufflés, Hot Chocolate	32
Steamed Chocolate Pudding with Apple and Raisin Topping	35
Torte, Chocolate and Raspberry	33
Torte, Chocolate Coconut	52
Torte, White Chocolate and Coffee	62
Trifle, Layered Chocolate	48
Truffle Slice, Chocolate	56
Truffles, Fresh Cream	15
Tuiles, Mini Chocolate	22
Upside-Down Cake, Sticky Blueberry	36
Walnut Pie, Chocolate	42
White Chocolate Clusters	26
White Chocolate Creams	47